DISCOVER EARTH SCIENCE

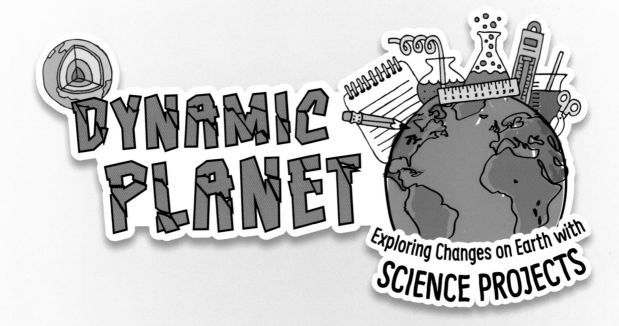

DYNAMIC PLANET

Exploring Changes on Earth with SCIENCE PROJECTS

by Tammy Enz

raintree

a Capstone company — publishers for children

Raintree is an imprint of Capstone Global Library Limited, a company incorporated in England and Wales having its registered office at 7 Pilgrim Street, London, EC4V 6LB – Registered company number: 6695582

www.raintree.co.uk
myorders@raintree.co.uk

Edited by Alesha Sullivan
Designed by Sarah Bennett
Picture research by Kelly Garvin
Production by Lori Barbeau

ISBN 978 1 474 70324 6
19 18 17 16 15
10 9 8 7 6 5 4 3 2 1

British Library Cataloguing in Publication Data
A full catalogue record for this book is available from the British Library.

Acknowledgements
Capstone Press/Karon Dubke, 8, 12, 13, 15, 18, 19, 21, 24, 28, 29; Shutterstock: beboy, cover, Budkov Denis, 6, daulon, 11, (bottom), 25 (inset), DavidMurk, 6 (inset), Designua, 9, Dmitry Naumov, 4–5, Doczky, 25, Igor Zh., 14, ixpert, 22–23, hans engbers, 16–17, Juancat, 7, Kingarion, 23 (bottom right), meunierd, 26–27, Tami Freed, 20, Wead, 10–11
Design Elements: Shutterstock: Curly Pat, Magnia, Markovka, Ms.Moloko, Orfeev, pockygallery, Sashatigar

We would like to thank Ginger L. Schmid, PhD, Associate Professor for the Department of Geography at Minnesota State University, Mankato, for her invaluable help in the preparation of this book.

Printed and bound in China.

Contents

Our lively planet

Many people think Earth is solid and unchanging. But it is constantly, often violently, changing. The solid ground we stand on is really a thin crust. Far beneath it Earth's core is intensely hot. Its heat melts parts of the rocky **mantle** below the crust. This **molten** material, pushing through the crust, causes quakes and massive eruptions. Earthquakes, volcanoes and underwater eruptions continually shape and change Earth's surface and coastlines.

Changes in weather and climate also alter **landscapes** and **biological** systems on our planet. Changing temperatures, rushing water and creeping glaciers have amazing Earth-changing powers.

Would you like to see close-up how Earth changes? Would you like to re-create some of Earth's amazing processes? With a few simple supplies, you can build your own miniature Earth-shattering projects. Some of these experiments may require an adult's help. Think safety first! And remember, science can sometimes be messy — so don't forget to tidy up when you've finished.

mantle layer of hot rock that surrounds Earth's core

molten melted by heat; lava is molten rock

landscape form of the land in a particular area

biology having to do with plant and animal life

5

Shaky ground!

Earth's surface is a thin rocky crust only about 40 kilometres (25 miles) thick on average. The crust is made of rocky plates. The plates float on a semi-molten crust. **Magma** seeps, oozes and erupts between plate edges.

As plate edges collide, their impact shakes the ground, causing earthquakes. As plates move apart, magma rises to form new landmasses and volcanic eruptions. If an earthquake or volcano happens on the ocean floor, a **tsunami** may occur.

The theory of **plate tectonics** describes the movement of Earth's plates and the reshaping of Earth's surface. Try this simple tasty project to see plate tectonics in action.

magma melted rock found beneath the surface of Earth

tsunami large, destructive wave caused by an underwater earthquake or volcano

plate tectonics scientific theory that Earth's surface is made of large plates that move very slowly

Growing discovery

A new island, called Niijima, was discovered in Japanese waters on 20 November, 2013. Over the next few weeks, volcanic action caused the island to quickly swell in size. The small island has continued expanding, overtaking a larger island near by. Niijima has grown to more than 1,000 metres (3,280 feet) across.

What you do

What you need

spoon

container of icing (red food colouring is optional)

tray bake tin

spatula

packet of square or rectangular biscuits

1. Use the spoon to scoop the icing into the tray bake tin. Smooth it out evenly across the bottom of the tin with a spatula.

2. Place the biscuits in a single layer over the icing. Cover the entire surface, making sure not to overlap the biscuit edges.

3. With your finger move a biscuit in any direction. What happens to the biscuits around it and to the icing below?

4. Using slightly more force, push several biscuits together.

What happened when some of the biscuit "plates" moved away from each other? What do you think will happen if the "magma" icing is exposed? In real life, when molten material bubbles up to the surface, it is called **lava**.

Theory of plate tectonics

Have you ever noticed how Earth's continents look as if they could fit together like pieces of a puzzle? Scientist Alfred Wegener theorized in 1915 that at one time all continents were part of a single landmass. He called this landmass Pangaea, meaning "all the lands". Wegener couldn't explain how the continents drifted apart. But scientists have since found evidence to support Wegener's theory. When studying ocean ridges, scientists have found lava spewing from the ocean floor. Over millions of years this action is responsible for pushing plates apart.

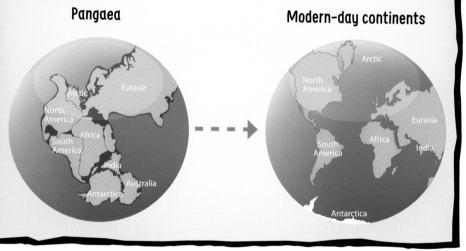

Pangaea

Modern-day continents

lava hot, liquid rock that pours out of a volcano when it erupts; lava is magma that reaches Earth's surface

Plugged up magma

Some volcanoes slowly ooze lava.
Some continuously erupt for years.
Others violently explode when a magma
plug causes a build-up of gases and lava. When
Mount St Helens in the western United States
violently erupted in 1980, it blew ash 18,300 metres
(60,000 ft) into the air. Would you like to build your own
volcano? Try this experiment in your garden and see
volcanic action up close!

As one plate slips below another, the grinding together of the plates produces earthquakes. Plate movement also causes magma to surface.

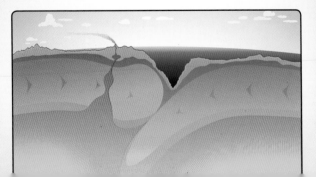

What you do

What you need

large, empty plastic bottle

half a raw potato

towel

measuring jug

white vinegar

bicarbonate of soda

three squares of toilet tissue

1. Remove the cap from the empty plastic bottle.

2. Make a cork by pushing and twisting the cut side of the potato onto the opening of the bottle. Push the potato onto the bottle about 5 centimetres (2 inches). Carefully remove the potato cork, and set aside.

3. Place a towel on an outdoor table and place the bottle in the middle of the towel.

4. Pour 480 millilitres of white vinegar into the bottle.

5. Put 5 grams (1 teaspoon) of bicarbonate of soda on the middle of each toilet tissue square. Roll the tissue around the bicarbonate of soda. Twist the ends to form a small packet.

6. Drop the bicarbonate of soda packets into the bottle. Quickly put the potato cork on the bottle, and take several steps away from the bottle. What happened inside and outside of the bottle? What happened to the potato cork? Does the explosion remind you of a volcano?

Major destruction

The most destructive volcano in recorded history was Mount Tambora in Indonesia in 1815. Continuously erupting for months, the volcano killed 90,000 people. The ash it spewed blocked the Sun, and the blockage changed Earth's climate. Thousands of miles away, Americans experienced midsummer snow and crop losses. Non-stop rain in Ireland and Great Britain led to crop failure, starvation and illness.

Tidal Waves

Volcanoes and earthquakes that happen under the sea cause different effects than those that occur on land. The underwater disruptions can cause tsunami that crash into coastlines and cause major damage. On average, two destructive tsunami occur every year across the world. See for yourself how tsunami work.

FACT

Tsunami can travel up to 800 kilometres (500 miles) per hour in deep ocean waters. The waves are about 1 metre (3 ft) high. Tsunami slow down as they approach land, and the waves get bigger. Some waves can reach up to 15 metres (50 ft) high!

What you do

1. Use the sand to build a mini beach about 5 centimetres (2 in) high along one end of the plastic container. The beach should extend across about one-quarter of the container.

2. Slowly pour water into the container opposite the beach until the water measures 2.5 centimetres (1 in) high.

3. Place the plastic trees and houses on the beach.

4. Gently blow on the surface of the water to create waves.

5. After creating some normal waves, grab the end of the container opposite the beach. Quickly jerk the box towards you. What happened to the trees and houses? Where did some of the sand move?

What you need

sand

plastic container measuring 30 x 60 centimetres (12 x 24 in) and at least 15 centimetres (6 in) deep

water

3 or 4 small plastic houses and trees

15

Wearing away the coast

Tsunami waves carry beach sand out into the water away from the coastline. But the everyday movement of water can also drastically eat away at landmasses. **Erosion** along rivers and coasts moves soil from one place to another, which greatly changes the landscape over time. Build your own coastline and see erosion at work with this experiment.

Caution: This is a messy project and should be done outside.

erosion   wearing away of land by water or wind

What you do

1. In the middle of one side of the cake tin, measure and mark a 1.25-centimetre (½-inch) diameter circle. The circle should be as close to the bottom of the tin as possible. Use the utility knife to cut out the circle.

What you need

disposable aluminum cake tin

ruler

pen

utility or craft knife

damp sand

handful of gravel or small rocks

small block of wood

bottle of water

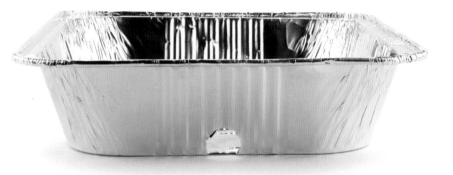

2. Spread damp sand across the bottom of the tin about 2.5 centimetres (1 in) high.

3. Use your fingers to dig a winding "river bed" in the sand from the hole to the opposite side of the tin. Your river should be about 2.5 centimetres (1 in) wide. Smooth and firm up the banks on both sides of the river.

4. Place several rocks along one of the bends in the river. Place several more along another bend.

5. Prop up the end of the tin opposite the hole on the block of wood.

Helpful Hint: You may need to place the tin on a flat board or book for stability.

6. Slowly pour the water into the river bed from the propped-up end of the tin. What's happening to the river's shoreline? Where is the **sediment** being carried? How do rocks along the river bends affect erosion?

sediment tiny bits of rock, shells, plants, sand and minerals that settle at the bottom of a liquid

vegetation plant life or the plants that cover an area

Freezing and thawing land

Believe it or not, resting water can change a landscape. Water expands when it freezes, so water can break large rocks apart. Water works its way into small cracks. When the water freezes it opens the cracks. Over a very long time, **weathering** caused by freezing and thawing can turn a mountain into a pile of gravel. Take an inside look at freezing and thawing using a few simple supplies.

FACT

The Appalachian Mountains in North America are considered to be old, eroding mountains. This range loses about 2 millimetres in height every hundred years.

weathering breaking down of solid rock into smaller and smaller pieces by wind, water, glaciers or plant roots

20

What you do

1. Fill a balloon with water until it starts to expand. Seal the balloon by tying off the end.

2. Measure and pour 114 grams of plaster of paris and 80 millilitres of water into the bowl. Stir with a plastic spoon.

Helpful Hint: Do not wash the spoon or bowl used to mix plaster in the sink. The plaster can harden inside the drain and cause damage.

3. Place the balloon into the plaster mixture in the bowl. Roll the balloon around until it is completely covered in plaster.

4. Let the plaster harden around the balloon inside the bowl for 30 minutes. When the plaster has hardened, put the bowl in the freezer.

5. Wait at least one hour before removing the bowl from the freezer. What's happened to the plaster?

What you need

balloon

water

measuring jug

plaster of paris

plastic, disposable bowl

plastic, disposable spoon

clock or timer

freezer

A gassy place

Gases in Earth's **atmosphere** change our planet's surface over time. Earth is like a giant greenhouse. Gardeners use greenhouses to grow plants in cool weather. The glass or plastic buildings allow the Sun's heat inside. The plants and ground inside the greenhouse warm up and give off **infrared rays**. But the rays can't escape back outside through the glass building. The rays bounce around and keep the greenhouse warm.

In the same way, the Sun's heat warms Earth. When the heat bounces back into space, gases in the atmosphere trap some of the heat. Without the gases Earth would be too cold. But too much of these gases can cause the planet to heat up. Now you can check out how the greenhouse effect works.

atmosphere   mixture of gases that surrounds Earth

infrared rays   heat rays; a form of radiation similar to visible light that is given off by all warm objects

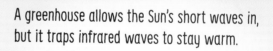

A greenhouse allows the Sun's short waves in, but it traps infrared waves to stay warm.

What you do

1. Pour 480 millilitres of water into each of the jars. Put three ice cubes in each of the jars. Put the lids onto the jars.

2. Put one of the jars inside the clear storage bag, and seal it.

3. Put both jars in a sunny place for an hour.

4. Use a thermometer to measure the temperature of the water inside each jar. What do you notice? Which jar's water has reached a higher temperature?

What you need

measuring jug

cold water

2 medium-sized jars with lids

ice cubes

large, clear storage bag

clock or timer

thermometer

Earth's rising temperatures

Scientists have been tracking Earth's average temperatures since the 1880s. Although Earth has gone through several warming and cooling cycles, it has warmed by about 0.5 degrees Celsius (1 degree Fahrenheit) in that time. The levels of **carbon dioxide**, a greenhouse gas, have also increased. Too much carbon dioxide gas released by cars and factories cause Earth to hold on to too much heat. The increase makes the planet warmer and this causes concern among many about Earth's future.

carbon dioxide   colourless, odourless gas that people and animals breathe out

Icy landscape

Glaciers have shaped much of the surface of Earth. The heavy sheets of ice flow across colder regions. When snow and ice add to a glacier's weight, they flow faster and grow larger. Melting causes them to shrink and pull back.

The moving ice sheets shove piles of rock into hills. They can also carve out deep valleys. Glaciers once covered the majority of Earth's surface. They are still at work in many places. Take a closer look at how glaciers work with this fun project!

glacier huge moving body of ice found in mountain valleys or polar regions

What you do

What you need

- sand
- small pebbles and stones
- tray bake tin
- notebook and pencil
- books
- ruler
- 2 full 118-millilitre bottles of white glue
- 2 bowls
- warm water
- 2 spoons
- measuring jug
- borax powder
- cling film
- tape

1. Spread a handful of sand, pebbles and stones evenly across the bottom of a tray bake tin. Using your notebook and pencil, sketch the location of the stones and pebbles.

2. Prop up one end of the pan on a stack of books about 7.5 centimetres (3 in) high.

3. Pour both bottles of glue into a bowl. Fill the empty glue bottles about half full with warm water. Shake the bottles well and then empty the bottles into the bowl.

4. Stir the glue mixture with a spoon.

5. Measure 120 millilitres of warm water into the other mixing bowl. Add 5 grams (1 teaspoon) borax powder. Stir together with the other spoon.

6. Pour the water and borax mixture into the bowl with the glue.

Ever-changing Earth

The planet we live on is constantly changing. The changes aren't always abrupt or powerful. Drops of water, invisible gases and underground plate movement are all causes of Earth's various changes. Look around you. You can see changes happening everywhere! Many of these changes are fundamental for life on Earth.

7. Stir about 10 times until a lumpy mixture begins to form. Quickly remove the lump, stretch it out and place it along the propped-up end of the cake tin. The mixture should be runny and wet.

8. Tightly cover the tin with cling film. To make the tin airtight, tape down the edges of the cling film.

9. Observe the glacier periodically for several hours. Leave it overnight. Frequently compare it to your sketch. How has the landscape changed? Does your glacier push some rocks and sand into piles?

Glossary

atmosphere   mixture of gases that surrounds Earth

biology   having to do with plant and animal life

carbon dioxide   colourless, odourless gas that people and animals breathe out

erosion   wearing away of land by water or wind

glacier   huge moving body of ice found in mountain valleys or polar regions

infrared rays   heat rays; a form of radiation similar to visible light that is given off by all warm objects

landscape   form of the land in a particular area

lava   hot, liquid rock that pours out of a volcano when it erupts; lava is magma that reaches Earth's surface

magma   melted rock found beneath the surface of Earth

mantle   layer of hot rock that surrounds Earth's core

molten   melted by heat; lava is molten rock

plate tectonics   scientific theory that the Earth's surface is made of large plates that move very slowly

sediment   tiny bits of rock, shells, plants, sand and minerals that settle at the bottom of a liquid

tsunami   large, destructive wave caused by an underwater earthquake or volcano

vegetation   plant life or the plants that cover an area

weathering   breaking down of solid rock into smaller and smaller pieces by wind, water, glaciers or plant roots

Read more

A Journey to the Centre of the Earth (Fantasy Field Trips), Claire Throp (Raintree, 2014)

Are Humans Damaging the Atmosphere? (Earth Debates), Catherine Chambers (Raintree, 2015)

Surviving Tsunami (Children's True Stories), Kevin Cunningham (Raintree, 2012)

Websites

www.bbc.co.uk/education/clips/zwwxn39
Short video clips that explore Earth and its natural processes.

http://ngkids.co.uk/science-and-nature/
Did you know that glacial ice often looks bright blue because the ice is so dense and compact? For more information about glaciers, volcanoes and earthquakes, plus some amazing photographs, visit the National Geographic children's website.

Index